THE REDEEMER

A MUSICAL JOURNEY THROUGH THE
LIFE OF **JESUS** THE **CHRIST**

JENNY OAKS BAKER

MUSIC BY KURT BESTOR · TEXT BY BRIAN CORDRAY

SHADOW
MOUNTAIN
PUBLISHING

Dedicated to Jesus Christ,

the Savior and Redeemer of the World

Music Credits

All arrangements by Kurt Bestor

"The Redeemer Overture," "Jesus' Baptism: Righteousness Fulfilled," "The Beatitudes: Blessed Be," "The Miracle of Lazarus: Come Forth," "The Redeemer Overture Reprise," "Gethsemane: From Every Pore," "Spirit World: In Paradiso," and "He Lives! Theme from *The Lamb of God*" composed by Kurt Bestor

"For unto Us a Child Is Born," "And the Glory of the Lord," and "Hallelujah Chorus" composed by George Frideric Handel

"God Loved Us, So He Sent His Son" composed by Alexander Schreiner

"Ave Maria" composed by J. S. Bach and Charles Gounod

"Come, Follow Me" composed by Samuel McBurney

"I Stand All Amazed" composed by Charles Gabriel

"O, Divine Redeemer" composed by Charles Gounod

"In Humility, Our Savior" composed by Rowland H. Prichard

"Upon the Cross of Calvary" composed by Leroy J. Robertson

"I Know That My Redeemer Lives" composed by Lewis D. Edwards

Text © 2025 Jenny Oaks Baker

Visit us at ShadowMountain.com

Library of Congress Cataloging-in-Publication Data

CIP on file

ISBN 978-1-63993-308-2

Printed in China

RR Donnelley, Dongguan, China

10 9 8 7 6 5 4 3 2 1

CONTENTS

INTRODUCTION

Throughout my life, I have strived to follow the Holy Spirit in my efforts to record and perform music that brings people closer to the Savior. Even though I have felt inspired in my previous musical projects, throughout the creation of *The Redeemer*, I have been continually stunned and thrilled by the clear ways that the Spirit has guided and directed each aspect of this glorious work.

The Redeemer began as an album for violin, orchestra, and choir. While composer Kurt Bestor and I were discussing various future album ideas, he suggested recording music entirely centered on Jesus Christ. The Spirit immediately and clearly manifested that this was exactly what the Lord wanted us to create for my next project. This was just the beginning of the inspiration and miracles that have flowed throughout the evolution of what has become *The Redeemer*.

As Kurt and I discussed the Savior's life, we knew immediately that the title and focus of my album was to be *The Redeemer*. We felt inspired as we selected ten of the most pivotal episodes of the Savior's life and chose either beloved hymns or original melodies to highlight each of these episodes. Beginning the album with "God Loved Us, So He Sent His Son" felt especially fitting to highlight God's infinite love for His children in sending His Only Begotten Son to Earth to make redemption possible for all. Divine guidance is apparent in the brilliant reworking of three classical masterpieces—Gounod's

"O Divine Redeemer" and two selections from Handel's *Messiah*. Kurt was also inspired in his emotional and stunning new original compositions, "Gethsemane: From Every Pore" and "Spirit World: In Paradiso." I personally feel that the music from *The Redeemer* is some of the most glorious and inspired music ever written!

The Redeemer album was released in March 2022, and Kurt and I performed the live album premier show in Rexburg, Idaho, in May with a cello soloist, choir, and orchestra. In planning this concert, I felt inspired to ask scriptwriter Brian Cordray to write introductions for each of the songs that would be accompanied by Bible video footage. We also added the encore "I Know that My Redeemer Lives" to end the work on a personal level for the performers and audience. As we performed this initial *The Redeemer* concert, I could sense that those in the audience were being deeply moved by the music, and I knew that God wanted me to share it far and wide to bring people closer to Jesus Christ. I then spent the next few years learning how to effectively produce concert tours to take *The Redeemer* and other Christ-centered shows throughout the world.

In the initial *The Redeemer* performances, I received many clear impressions on how to expand and improve the work. These ideas included commissioning Kurt to compose eight additional movements to highlight even more of the Savior's life and mission (including a gorgeous original baptism movement, and a gloriously rearranged Hallelujah Chorus movement to represent the Ascension); asking Kurt to add vocal soloist parts to some of the movements to enhance the production's emotional impact; and adding live narration to the show to further testify of the Savior's divine mission.

I feel very humbled and grateful every time I hear or perform *The Redeemer*. The inspired music profoundly touches my soul. It fills me with increased love for our Savior and appreciation that He was willing to die for us so we can live again. I am so grateful for the many miracles and blessings that have enabled us to bring this music to so many of God's children, and I hope that this production brings everyone who experiences it closer to the Savior. I know that Jesus Christ lives, and that He truly is our Redeemer!

JENNY OAKS BAKER

PROLOGUE

If you could visit any moment in human history, where would you decide to go? The world has certainly seen its share of memorable moments: heroic deeds, stirring speeches, technological achievements, and social advancements. Nevertheless, one occasion surpasses them all in terms of eternal significance: We joyfully proclaim that the most momentous event in history occurred nearly 2,000 years ago when our Redeemer knelt in the Garden of Gethsemane to suffer as a ransom for our sins and three days later was gloriously resurrected. We wish to symbolically revisit sacred scenes from our Savior's eternal ministry through holy scripture and inspired music. Our hope is that throughout this musical journey, we might each draw closer to Jesus Christ.

The Redeemer Overture

Shma Israel Adonai Elohenu Adonai enu.
Shma Israel Elohim.
Elohenu Adonai ehad baruch Elohenu.
Adonai ehad baruch haolam.
Elohenu Adonai ehad baruch Elohenu Adonai.
Elohenu Adonai ehad melich haolam!
Olam! Olam! Olam!
Hallelujah. Hallelujah.

—Kurt Bestor

Scan to listen to performance

THE CHOSEN: GOD LOVED US, SO HE SENT HIS SON

The scriptural record of Jesus Christ does not commence with the First Noël. Christ "verily was foreordained before the foundation of the world" (1 Peter 1:20) to save us from sin and death. Because God knows we will all sin during our earthly existence, He knows that we will need a Redeemer to atone for our sins. But who can do this? Thankfully, Jesus Christ unselfishly offers to pay the price for us. And because God so loves us, He sends His Son.

God Loved Us, So He Sent His Son

God loved us, so he sent his Son,
Christ Jesus, the atoning One,
To show us by the path he trod
The one and only way to God.

He came as man, though Son of God,
And bowed himself beneath the rod.
He died in holy innocence,
A broken law to recompense.

Oh, love effulgent, love divine!
What debt of gratitude is mine,
That in his off'ring I have part
And hold a place within his heart.

—Edward P. Kimball (1882–1937)

Scan to listen to performance

THE ANNUNCIATION: AVE MARIA

Our biblical account of the Annunciation to Mary provides remarkable insight into the character of this most noble daughter of God. Imagine one so young trying to comprehend the responsibility to not only bear, but raise as her own, the Savior of all mankind. Her willingness to submit to this foreordained call is a lesson in true discipleship for us all: "Behold the handmaid of the Lord; be it unto me according to thy word" (Luke 1:38).

Ave Maria

Ave Maria
Gratia plena
Dominus tecum
Benedicta tu in mulieribus
Et benedictus fructus ventris tui, Jesus.
Sancta Maria, Sancta Maria
Ora pro nobis
Nobis peccatoribus
Nunc et in hora
In hora mortis nostrae
Amen Amen.

Scan to listen to performance

BORN THIS DAY: FOR UNTO US A CHILD IS BORN

Perhaps no other story in holy scripture is as beautiful and beloved as the birth of Jesus Christ. Although He is born to a mortal mother, Jesus Christ is the Son of God. He came into our world as an infant, but was destined to redeem us from death and to open the door that we may all be resurrected and gain eternal life. "For unto us a child is born, unto us a son is given" (Isaiah 9:6).

For unto Us a Child Is Born

For unto us a child is born,
Unto us a son is given:
And the government shall be upon his shoulder:
And his name shall be called
Wonderful, Counsellor,
The mighty God, The everlasting Father,
The Prince of Peace.

—Isaiah 9:6

Scan to listen to performance

JESUS' BAPTISM: RIGHTEOUSNESS FULFILLED

Jesus Christ would teach through personal example that all must be baptized. Scripture testifies that the Savior came up from Galilee to Jordan unto John to be baptized. We can understand His cousin's initial reluctance—he knows all too well that there is one "mightier than [he], whose shoes [he is] not worthy to bear" (Matthew 3:11). And yet, Jesus gently exhorts him: "Suffer it to be so now: for thus it becometh us to fulfil all righteousness" (Matthew 3:15). As the Lord emerges "straightway" from the water the heavens open, the Spirit of God descends like a dove, and a voice from above declares: "This is my beloved Son, in whom I am well pleased" (Matthew 3:16–17).

Jesus' Baptism: Righteousness Fulfilled

Repent ye! Repent ye! For the kingdom of Heaven is at hand.
Prepare ye. Preparing to make the path before Him straight.
I call all to repentance to the water.
But He who follows me will baptize you
With the Holy Ghost and fire.

Baptize me.
I'm not worthy.
Why comest Thou to me? I should be sanctified by thee.
Baptize me.
I am not worthy to bear Thy shoes.
Baptize me so righteousness might be fulfilled.
Thy will be done.
Elahi, Elahi, Elahi bar Adam.
In the name of the Father and of the Son and of the Holy Ghost
    I baptize you.
Talyâ d'alla âhâ
In the name of the Father and of the Son and of the Holy Spirit
    I baptize you.
Amen.

And then the heavens were opened
Descended from high like a dove,
The Holy Spirit of Promise upon the Son,
The anointed one upon Him shown.
'Tis my beloved in whom I am well pleased.

—Kurt Bestor

Scan to listen to performance

FISHERS OF MEN: COME, FOLLOW ME

Imagine the frustration of several experienced fishermen as they return from a night of backbreaking work empty-handed. While they clean and repair their nets, Jesus Christ teaches a crowd of people gathered on the shore. Afterward, He instructs the exhausted men to again cast their nets. They see no point in doing so—after all, they haven't caught a single fish all night. Yet obediently, they lower their nets into the water . . . where, miraculously, they are blessed with so many fish that they have to ask their associates for help so that the boat doesn't sink. After they return to shore, Jesus then asks these men to do something that will require even greater faith than simply casting nets—He invites them to come unto Him so He can make them fishers of men. "And they straightway left their nets, and followed him" (Matthew 4:20).

Come, Follow Me

"Come, follow me," the Savior said.
Then let us in his footsteps tread,
For thus alone can we be one
With God's own loved, begotten Son.

"Come, follow me," a simple phrase,
Yet truth's sublime, effulgent rays
Are in these simple words combined
To urge, inspire the human mind.

Is it enough alone to know
That we must follow him below,
While trav'ling thru this vale of tears?
No, this extends to holier spheres.

Not only shall we emulate
His course while in this earthly state,
But when we're freed from present cares,
If with our Lord we would be heirs.

We must the onward path pursue
As wider fields expand to view,
And follow him unceasingly,
Whate'er our lot or sphere may be.

For thrones, dominions, kingdoms, pow'rs,
And glory great and bliss are ours,
If we, throughout eternity,
Obey his words, "Come, follow me."

—John Nicholson (1839–1909)

Scan to listen to performance

WOMAN AT THE WELL: I STAND ALL AMAZED

In ancient times, Jewish men were forbidden to discuss theological matters with women. Furthermore, Samaritans were branded as outcasts and impure, compelling most observant Jews to avoid traveling through Samaria whenever possible. Imagine, then, the sheer amazement of a Samaritan woman at a well as she suddenly finds herself alone with the Savior. Although aware of her sinful past, He asks her for water and then offers her "Living Water" in return. Throughout His mortal ministry, Jesus Christ demonstrates a perfect love for all of God's children. As His disciples today, we too can stand all amazed that "God is no respecter of persons: But in every nation he that feareth him, and worketh righteousness, is accepted with him" (Acts 10:34–35).

I Stand All Amazed

I stand all amazed at the love Jesus offers me,
Confused at the grace that so fully he proffers me.
I tremble to know that for me he was crucified,
That for me, a sinner, he suffered, he bled and died.

Oh, it is wonderful that he should care for me
Enough to die for me!
Oh, it is wonderful, wonderful to me!

I marvel that he would descend from his throne divine
To rescue a soul so rebellious and proud as mine,
That he should extend his great love unto such as I,
Sufficient to own, to redeem, and to justify.

Oh, it is wonderful that he should care for me
Enough to die for me!
Oh, it is wonderful, wonderful to me!

I think of his hands pierced and bleeding to pay the debt!
Such mercy, such love and devotion can I forget?
No, no, I will praise and adore at the mercy seat,
Until at the glorified throne I kneel at his feet.

Oh, it is wonderful that he should care for me
Enough to die for me!
Oh, it is wonderful, wonderful to me!

—Charles H. Gabriel (1856–1932)

Scan to listen to performance

MARY MAGDALENE: O DIVINE REDEEMER

Mary Magdalene is an example of abiding faith as one of Christ's most devoted disciples. As reported by both Mark and Luke, she had been possessed of seven devils until the Savior mercifully cast them out. This compassionate act left her with an unshakable testimony of the Lord's love, power, and grace. She consequently follows Jesus for the rest of His earthly mission—even choosing to remain with Him as He suffers and dies on the cross, and assisting in His subsequent burial in the tomb. Then, on that glorious Easter morning, Mary's devotion leads her back to His now empty tomb where she is blessed with the honor of being the first person to witness the Divine Redeemer in His resurrected state.

O Divine Redeemer

Ah! Turn me not away,
Receive me tho' unworthy,
Hear Thou my cry,
Behold, Lord, my distress!

Answer me from thy throne
Haste Thee, Lord, to mine aid,
Thy pity show in my deep anguish!

Let not the sword of vengeance smite me,
Tho' righteous thine anger, O Lord!
Shield me in danger, O regard me!
On Thee, Lord, alone will I call.

O Divine Redeemer!
I pray Thee, grant me pardon,
And remember not, remember not, O Lord, my sins!

Night gathers round my soul;
Fearful, I cry to Thee;
Come to mine aid, O Lord!
Haste Thee, Lord, haste to help me!

Hear my cry! Save me Lord in Thy mercy;
Hear my cry! Come and save me, O Lord!

O Divine Redeemer!
I pray Thee, grant me pardon,
And remember not, remember not, O Lord, my sins!

Save, in the day of retribution,
From Death shield Thou me, O my God!
O Divine Redeemer, have mercy!
Help me, my Saviour!

—Charles Gounod (1818–1893)

Scan to listen to performance

THE BEATITUDES: BLESSED BE

While the world has certainly had its share of wise and effective teachers across the ages, all pale in comparison to Jesus Christ. Of His countless sermons, teachings, and lessons—some given to large groups of people, others conducted one-on-one—the Sermon on the Mount is one of Christ's greatest and provides all those desiring to follow Him with a comprehensive outline for righteous living. Containing what is known today as the Beatitudes, the Lord's instruction helps His disciples understand blessings that Heavenly Father has in store for the faithful, in this life and in the world to come. Indeed, "blessed be" those who hearken and obey the Master Teacher.

The Beatitudes: Blessed Be

Blessed, how blessed be
Thus saith the Lord.
Oh how blessed are the poor in spirit
For theirs is the kingdom of Heaven.
Oh how blessed are the poor in spirit.
How blessed, blessed.
How blessed saith the Lord.
Oh blessed are they who mourn
For they all will be comforted.
How blessed, blessed
Thus saith the Lord.
Blessed be all those that are meek;
They shall inherit the earth.
Blessed are those who hunger and thirst for righteousness
For they will be satisfied.
Oh how blessed are they who are merciful
For they will be shown His mercy.

And blessed are the pure in heart
For they will see God.
And blessed are the peacemakers
For they will be called the sons of God.
And blessed are those who are persecuted for righteousness
For theirs is the kingdom of Heaven.
Thus saith the Lord.
Blessed, blessed.
Thus saith the Lord.

—Kurt Bestor

Scan to listen to performance

THE MIRACLE OF LAZARUS: COME FORTH

All can be touched by the endearing love of two sisters for their ailing brother. As the account reads, Mary and Martha send word to Jesus of Larazus's failing health. However, before the Lord comes to heal him, the brother dies. "Too late," the people surely think. "If only Christ had arrived sooner." Although the Redeemer knows that the separation between these beloved siblings will only be temporary, He demonstrates His all-compassionate heart by weeping with them in their hour of grief. "Behold, how He loved him" (John 11:36), the people declare. And now the miracle: the Savior awakens Lazarus out of death's sleep by first commanding that the stone be removed from its place, and then calling for his beloved friend to "come forth" (John 11:43).

Scan to listen to performance

THE KING RETURNS: AND THE GLORY OF THE LORD

Join me now as we visit the last week of the Messiah's mortal ministry. It begins on the Sunday before Passover—the day the paschal lambs are traditionally brought into Jerusalem from the fields of Bethlehem for sacrifice. The symbolism could not be more perfect as Jesus, the Lamb of God, born in the City of David, now enters triumphantly into Jerusalem. He is well aware of the significance of His arrival. The Advent of "the King of Kings into His royal city" serves as the fulfillment of Zechariah's grand prophecy: "Rejoice greatly, O daughter of Zion; shout, O daughter of Jerusalem: behold, thy King cometh unto thee" (Zechariah 9:9).

And the Glory of the Lord

And the glory of the Lord shall be revealed,
And all flesh shall see it together:
For the mouth of the Lord hath spoken it.

—Isaiah 40:5

Scan to listen to performance

The Redeemer Overture Reprise

Scan to listen to performance

THE LAST SUPPER: IN HUMILITY, OUR SAVIOR

Our journey now takes us to the final evening of the Savior's life. Mere hours before He is to begin the agonizing process of the Atonement, the Lord meets with His disciples to partake of the Feast of the Passover. He introduces the sacrament of the Lord's Supper by saying, "This is my body which is given for you: this do in remembrance of me. . . . This cup is the new testament in my blood, which is shed for you" (Luke 22:19–20). He then gives His concluding and perhaps most profound teaching in mortality: "A new commandment I give unto you, that ye love one another; as I have loved you, that ye also love one another. By this shall all men know that ye are my disciples, if ye have love one to another" (John 13:34–35).

In Humility, Our Savior

In humility, our Savior,
Grant thy Spirit here, we pray,
As we bless the bread and water
In thy name this holy day.
Let me not forget, O Savior,
Thou didst bleed and die for me
When thy heart was stilled and broken
On the cross at Calvary.

Fill our hearts with sweet forgiving;
Teach us tolerance and love.
Let our prayers find access to thee
In thy holy courts above.
Then, when we have proven worthy
Of thy sacrifice divine,
Lord, let us regain thy presence;
Let thy glory round us shine.

—Mabel Jones Gabbott (1910–2004)

Scan to listen to performance

GETHSEMANE: FROM EVERY PORE

The hour has now come for the Savior to perform His atoning sacrifice. In Gethsemane, Jesus Christ submits to the will of the Father and takes upon Himself the sins of all people. His suffering caused Him to pray, "Father, if thou be willing, remove this cup from me: nevertheless not my will, but thine, be done. And there appeared an angel unto him from heaven, strengthening him. And being in an agony he prayed more earnestly: and his sweat was as it were great drops of blood falling down to the ground" (Luke 22:42–44).

Scan to listen to performance

CRUCIFIXION: UPON THE CROSS OF CALVARY

Following the Savior's incomprehensible suffering in Gethsemane, He is then "arrested and condemned on spurious charges, convicted to satisfy a mob, and sentenced to die on Calvary's cross" ("The Living Christ"). Our Redeemer willingly allows Himself to suffer for all. Yet to add to that suffering, in those final excruciating moments, Heavenly Father briefly withdraws the comfort of His Spirit from His Perfect Son, so that He can fully understand how it feels to not only die physically, but spiritually. For that reason, we reverently sing: "Upon the cross of Calvary, they crucified our Lord and sealed with blood the sacrifice that sanctified His word."

Upon the Cross of Calvary

Upon the cross of Calvary
They crucified our Lord
And sealed with blood the sacrifice
That sanctified his word.

Upon the cross he meekly died
For all mankind to see
That death unlocks the passageway
Into eternity.

Upon the cross our Savior died,
But, dying, brought new birth
Through resurrection's miracle
To all the sons of earth.

—Vilate Raile (1890–1954)

Scan to listen to performance

SPIRIT WORLD: IN PARADISO

What happens between the Savior's death on the cross and His glorious Resurrection? Prophets and scripture testify that He visited the spirit world to minister to the obedient souls who lived hundreds, even thousands of years before Him. And why? To mercifully offer salvation to all those who have died that never had the chance to hear the gospel or to choose baptism. In this way, the opportunity for eternal life is finally available to all.

Scan to listen to performance

HE LIVES! THEME FROM *THE LAMB OF GOD*

He is not here: for He is risen" (Matthew 28:6). Those simple words, mouthed by an angel, announce the most extraordinary occurrence in recorded history: the Resurrection of Jesus Christ. Death is now conquered for all! Who can blame His humble disciples for initially struggling to grasp the reality of this most miraculous event? But their doubt quickly turns to joy as the Risen Lord appears to them, shows them the wounds in His hands, feet, and side, and speaks the words, "Peace be unto you" (John 20:26). His apostles became witnesses of the living Son of God throughout the world. As Jesus told his disciples, "If [anyone] will come after me, let [them] deny [themselves], and take up [their] cross, and follow me" (Matthew 16:24). Each of us must decide whether we will choose to embrace the Great Redeemer's infinite atonement and seek eternal life—for truly, He lives!

Scan to listen to performance

THE ASCENSION: HALLELUJAH CHORUS

Hallelujah! Hallelujah!
For the Lord God omnipotent reigneth.

Hallelujah! Hallelujah!

The kingdom of this world is become
the kingdom of our Lord, and of His Christ, and of His Christ;
And He shall reign for ever and ever,
King of kings, and Lord of lords.

King of kings, and Lord of lords. King of kings, and Lord of lords,
and He shall reign,
and He shall reign for ever and ever, for ever and ever,
Hallelujah! Hallelujah!

And He shall reign for ever and ever, for ever and ever.

King of kings! and Lord of lords!
King of kings! and Lord of lords!

And He shall reign for ever and ever,
King of kings! and Lord of lords! Hallelujah! Hallelujah!

—George Frideric Handel (1685–1759)

Scan to listen to performance

EPILOGUE

I Know That My Redeemer Lives

I know that my Redeemer lives.
What comfort this sweet sentence gives!
He lives, he lives, who once was dead.
He lives, my ever-living Head.
He lives to bless me with his love.
He lives to plead for me above.
He lives my hungry soul to feed.
He lives to bless in time of need.

He lives to grant me rich supply.
He lives to guide me with his eye.
He lives to comfort me when faint.
He lives to hear my soul's complaint.
He lives to silence all my fears.
He lives to wipe away my tears.
He lives to calm my troubled heart.
He lives all blessings to impart.

He lives, my kind, wise heav'nly Friend.
He lives and loves me to the end.
He lives, and while he lives, I'll sing.
He lives, my Prophet, Priest, and King.
He lives and grants me daily breath.
He lives, and I shall conquer death.
He lives my mansion to prepare.
He lives to bring me safely there.

He lives! All glory to his name!
He lives, my Savior, still the same.
Oh, sweet the joy this sentence gives:
"I know that my Redeemer lives!"
He lives! All glory to his name!
He lives, my Savior, still the same.
Oh, sweet the joy this sentence gives:
"I know that my Redeemer lives!"

—Samuel Medley (1738–1799)

Scan to listen to performance

Performance Credits

Producers: Jenny Oaks Baker and Kurt Bestor

Recording Engineers: Michael Gibbons, Stoker White, and Michael Greene

Soloists:

Violin: Jenny Oaks Baker

Cello: Sarah Noelle Baker

Piano: Hannah Jean Baker

Soprano: Lisa Hopkins Seegmiller

Tenor: Dallyn Vail Bayles

Bass: Preston Yates

Conductor: Kurt Bestor

Thank you to King and Diane Husein for helping to make this project possible!

Book Credits

Artwork Consultants: Mark and Julie Magleby

Book Editors: Jenny Oaks Baker and Hannah Baker

Copyeditor: Derk Koldewyn

Art Director: Garth Bruner

Typesetter: Breanna Anderl

Image Credits

P. iv—*Light of Life* © Annie Henrie Nader; used by permission.

P. 5—*Christ Blessing the Little Child* by Carl Heinrich Bloch; p. 9—*The Christus* by Bertel Thorvaldsen; photo by Jared Davies; p. 11—*The Annunciation* by John William Waterhouse; pp. 14–15—*Rest on the Flight into Egypt* by Luc-Oliver Merson; pp. 20–21—*Christ Calling the Apostles James and John* by Edward Armitage; p. 24—*Woman at the Well* by Carl Heinrich Bloch; p. 28—*The Conversion of Mary Magdalene* by Paolo Veronese; p. 32—*The Sermon on the Mount* by Carl Heinrich Bloch; p. 36—*The Raising of Lazarus* by Carl Heinrich Bloch; pp. 40–41—*Entry of Christ into Jerusalem* by Jean-Hippolyte Flandrin; p. 42—*Christ Walking on the Water* by Julius Sergius von Klever; pp. 46–47—*The Last Supper* by Pascal Dagnan-Bouveret; p. 48—*Agony in the Garden* by Frans Schwartz; p. 51—*The Crucifixion* by Francisco de Zurbarán; p. 52—*Resurrection of Christ* by Carl Heinrich Bloch / all courtesy Alamy Stock Photo

P. 12—*Bearing a Child in Her Arms* © Elspeth C. Young; used by permission.

P. 16—*John Baptizes Christ* by Harry Anderson © By Intellectual Reserve, Inc.; used by permission; p. 55—*Mary and the Resurrected Lord* by Harry Anderson © By Intellectual Reserve, Inc.; used by permission; p. 56—*The Second Coming* by Harry Anderson © By Intellectual Reserve, Inc.; used by permission.